Karel Husa

CONCERTO FOR VIOLIN AND ORCHESTRA

(Piano Reduction and Part)

AMP 8181

First printing: November, 2004

ISBN 0-634-05509-7

Associated Music Publishers, Inc.

DISTRIBUTED BY

HAL•LEONARD®
CORPORATION

7777 W. BLUEMOUND RD. P.O. BOX 13819 MILWAUKEE, WI 53213

*Husa's Concerto for Violin and Orchestra was commissioned by
the New York Philharmonic for its 150th Anniversary
and given its premiere performance by the New York Philharmonic
under the direction of Kurt Masur with Glenn Dicterow, violin, on May 27, 1993
at Avery Fisher Hall, Lincoln Center for the Performing Arts*

The violin was the first instrument I learned as a boy. My parents had given me one for Christmas and I immediately began lessons. My parents guided me toward engineering later on, but the War forced the closing of my school soon after I entered in 1939 and I was able to put my musical background to good use. The Conservatory had remained open so I applied and was accepted. Music was to become my profession.

The literature for violin is so rich that it is extremely difficult to add another work to the canon. A concerto, which traditionally tests the virtuosity of a soloist, is even more daunting to consider. Today's performers are technically amazing — what was considered difficult one hundred years ago is now being played regularly by students in Conservatory. Many pieces which seemed unplayable sixty years ago (such as the Bartók, Berg, and Stravinsky concerti) are performed masterfully today. Every period brings its new challenges and technical innovations.

However, technical challenges should not be the main concern of a composer. Ideas and content—sometimes called inspiration—are more important. These are more difficult to describe as they are personal matters which composers are often reluctant to discuss. Perhaps it would be more helpful to speak of the thoughts I had while creating this concerto.

We live in a world of many societies, yet more than ever there is a feeling of aloneness among people (Moderato, ma deciso—a monologue and recitative). We can see the Earth from a spaceship or another planet but we have not been able to stop hungry children from dying nor the destruction of our glorious natural resources (Adagio). Yet still we stop to contemplate life's mystery and beauty, its joy, its lights and darknesses, its magnificent colors (like the forests of Douanier Rousseau or the flight of birds painted by Chagall). In these troubled times we have much to learn from the majesty of Nature (Allegro giocoso).

–Karel Husa

INSTRUMENTATION

3 Flutes (3rd doubling Piccolo)
2 Oboes
English Horn
2 Clarinets in B♭
Bass Clarinet
2 Bassoons
Contrabassoon

4 Horns in F
3 Trumpets in C
3 Trombones
Tuba

Timpani

Percussion (3 players)
2 Harps

Solo Violin

Strings

duration ca. 28 minutes

Performance material is available on rental from the publisher.
G. Schirmer/AMP Rental and Performance Department
P.O. Box 572
Chester, NY 10918
(845) 469-4699 - phone
(845) 469-7544 - fax
www.schirmer.com

CONCERTO FOR VIOLIN AND ORCHESTRA

I

Karel Husa

* keep the same interval between the fingers (lower pitch
  is exact; upper pitch progressively slightly higher)

II

20

* depress this chord without sounding.

attacca

III

Allegro giocoso ♩ = 120

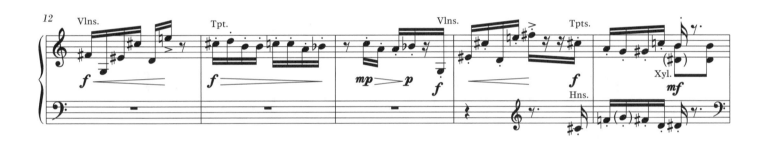

Violin

CONCERTO FOR VIOLIN AND ORCHESTRA

I

Karel Husa

* keep the same distance between the fingers (lower pitch
  is exact; upper note progressively slightly higher)

II

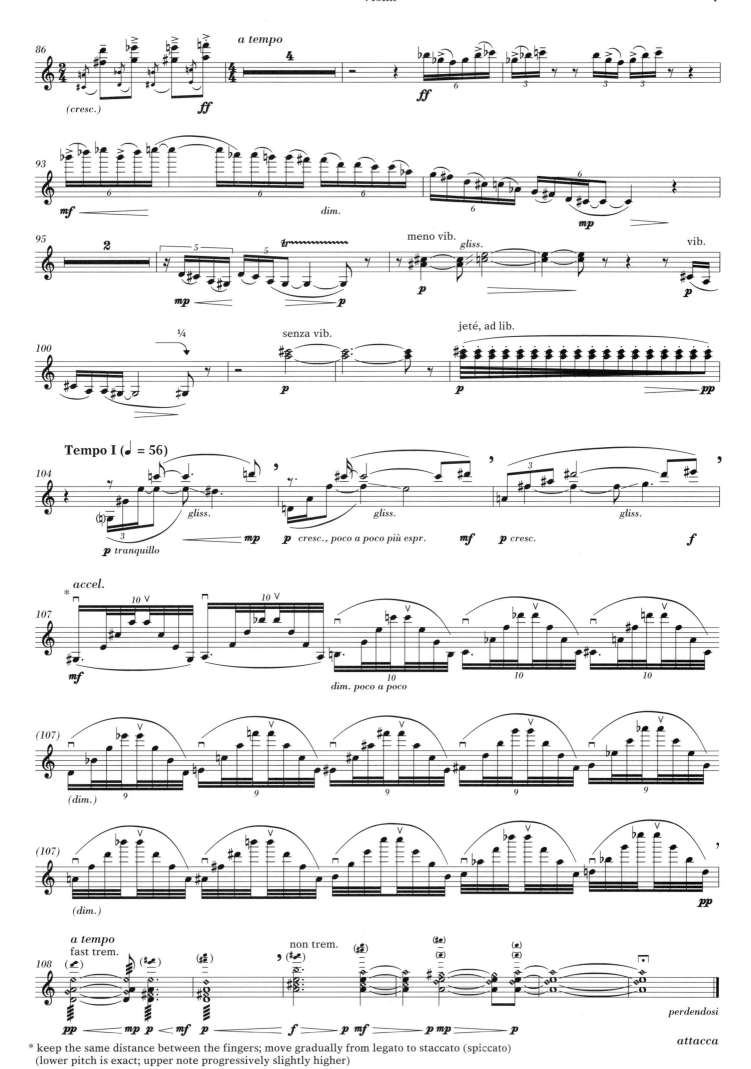

* keep the same distance between the fingers; move gradually from legato to staccato (spiccato)
(lower pitch is exact; upper note progressively slightly higher)

III

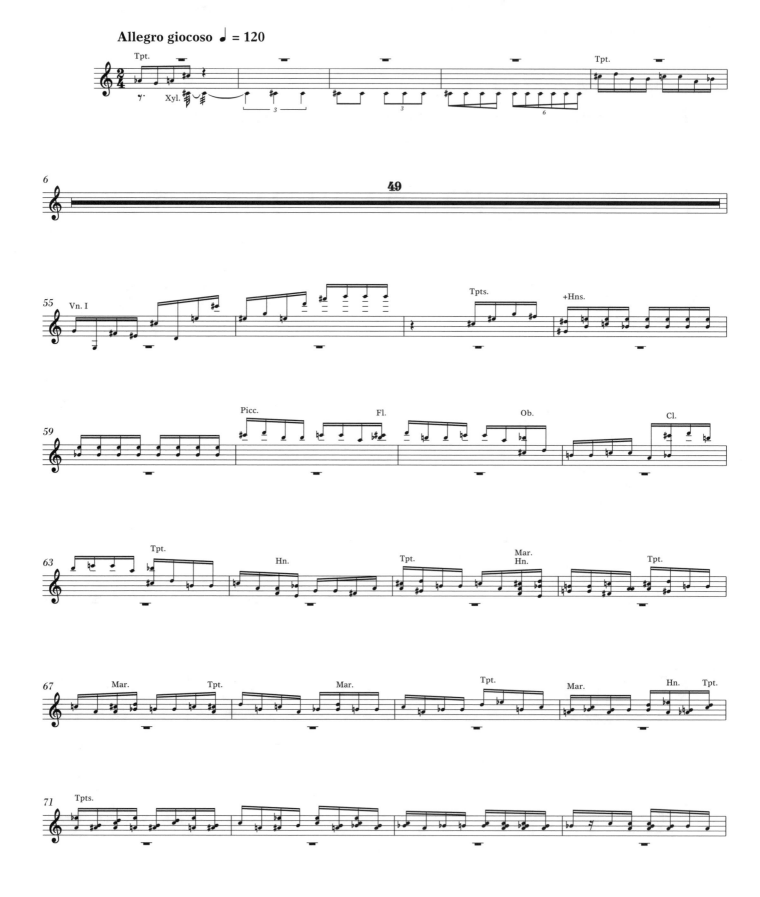

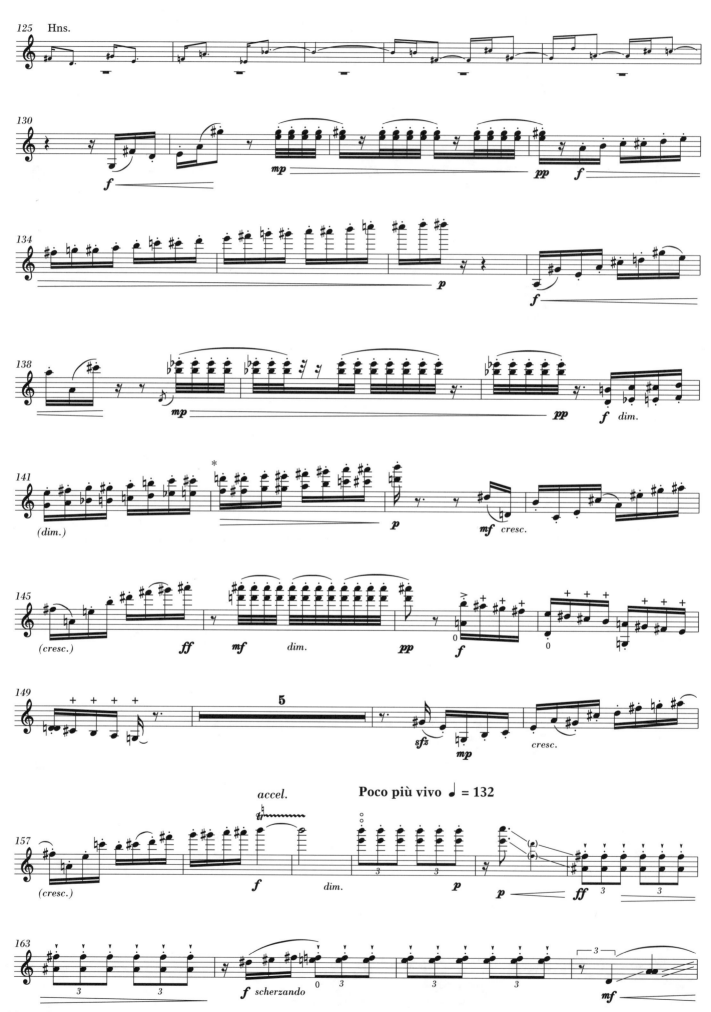

* keep the same distance between the fingers (lower pitch is exact, upper note progressively slightly higher)

Violin

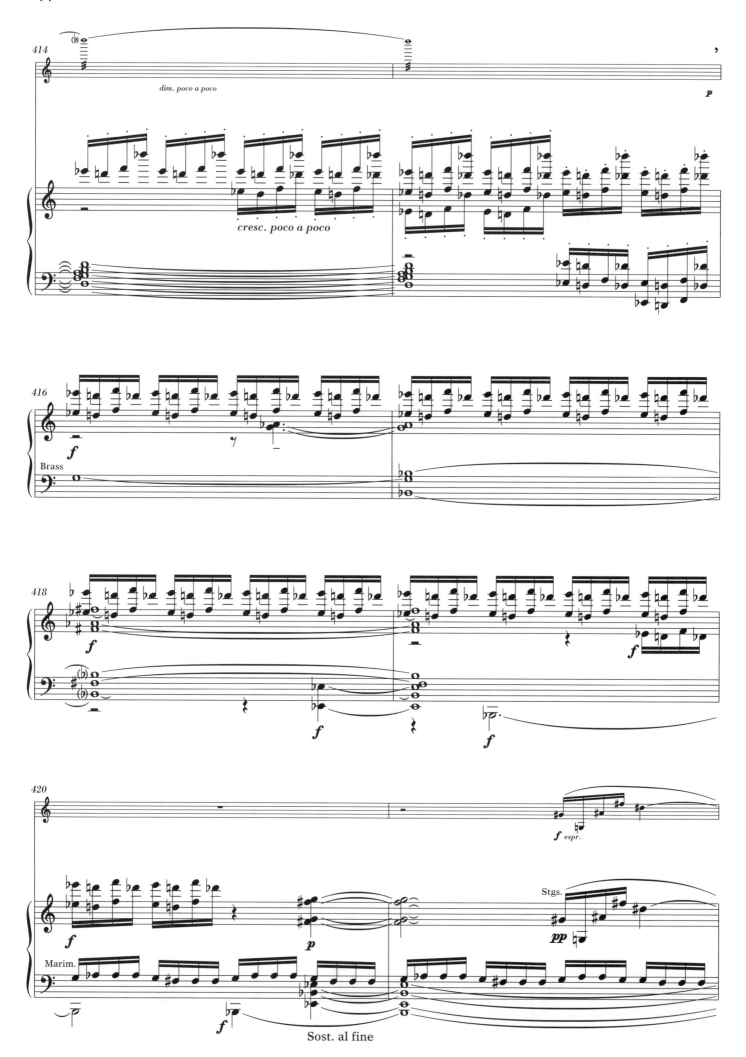